SEATTLE SOUNDERS

SOCCER CHAMPIONS

JEFF SAVAGE

LERNER PUBLICATIONS ◆ MINNEAPOLIS

Lerner Publications Company
A division of Lerner Publishing Group, Inc.
241 First Avenue North
Minneapolis, MN 55401 USA

For reading levels and more information, look up this title at www.lernerbooks.com.

Main body text set in Adrianna Regular.
Typeface provided by Chank.

Library of Congress Cataloging-in-Publication Data

Names: Savage, Jeff, 1961– author.
Title: Seattle Sounders : soccer champions / Jeff Savage.
Description: Minneapolis : Lerner Publications, [2018] | Series: Champion Soccer Clubs | Includes webography. | Includes bibliographical references and index.
Identifiers: LCCN 2017047421 (print) | LCCN 2017056531 (ebook) | ISBN 9781541525535 (eb pdf) | ISBN 9781541519909 (library binding : alk. paper) | ISBN 9781541527966 (paperback : alk. paper)
Subjects: LCSH: Seattle Sounders FC (Soccer team)—History—Juvenile literature. | Soccer players—Biography—Juvenile literature.
Classification: LCC GV943.6.S43 (ebook) | LCC GV943.6.S43 S39 2018 (print) | DDC 796.334/6309797772—dc23

LC record available at https://lccn.loc.gov/2017047421

Manufactured in the United States of America
1-44326-34572-1/9/2018

CONTENTS

INTRODUCTION
WHAT A COMEBACK!

The crowd at CenturyLink Field was rocking. The hometown Seattle Sounders trailed 2–0 at halftime. But the fans were singing: "We love you, Sounders. Hey! Ho! Sounders, we love you!" They believed their team could come back to win the game against D.C. United.

The Sounders were used to winning. They were the defending Major League Soccer (MLS) champions. But they were struggling in this 2017 MLS game.

Joevin Jones plays defense for the Sounders. In 2017, he made 13 assists.

The Seattle Sounders have some of the most loyal and passionate fans in the United States.

When United scored a third goal to start the second half, it looked hopeless. In nearly 5,000 games, no team in MLS history had ever come back from three goals behind to win.

The Sounders stayed focused. Joevin Jones kicked the ball hard toward the goal. Will Bruin headed it sideways past the D.C. United goalkeeper and into the net. The Sounders had finally scored.

About 10 minutes later, Jones flicked the ball with his left foot. Brad Evans jumped into the air and blasted the ball off his head for the goal. Suddenly it was 3–2.

In 2017, star midfielder Nicolas Lodeiro scored 7 goals and made 14 assists for Seattle.

The Sounders needed one more goal to tie. In the final minutes of the second half, Nicolas Lodeiro passed to Gustav Svensson, who kicked it into the goal for the tie!

Time was running out. The Sounders created one more chance. Bruin stole the ball and kicked it ahead to Cristian Roldan. Roldan caught up with it and got past a defender. Roldan blasted a shot between the legs of the goalkeeper into the net! "I shot as hard as I could . . . ," Roldan said. "And luckily, it went in." The Sounders won, 4–3, and made history.

Roldan's goal against D.C. United was his third goal of the season. He scored 6 goals total in 2017.

1

A WINNING START

The Sounders have been winners from the start. MLS was founded in 1996 with 10 teams. Over the years, the league added more and more teams. Seattle joined MLS in 2009 to become the league's 15th team. They were officially called Seattle Sounders FC. FC stands for Football Club. Soccer is known as football in most of the world.

Most MLS teams play in small stadiums built specifically for soccer. But the Sounders wanted to play in a big stadium. They knew people in the Pacific Northwest love soccer. Paul Allen, one of the new owners, is a billionaire who also owns the Seattle Seahawks, a National Football League (NFL) team. The Seahawks agreed to allow the Sounders to play their games at the Seahawks' home Qwest Field (later called CenturyLink Field) for free. It was a smart decision. They offered 22,000 season tickets for sale. The tickets sold out.

Qwest Field was renamed CenturyLink Field in 2011.

Sigi Schmid

The Sounders hired MLS legend Sigi Schmid to coach the team. He had won the **MLS Cup** a year earlier with the Columbus Crew, and he was about to set the league record for most all-time wins as a coach in MLS. Schmid was thrilled with his new job. "It's definitely the best situation I have been in," he said.

On March 19, 2009, the Sounders were ready for their first game. Team owners and the Seattle mayor led thousands of people in a parade to the stadium. More than 30,000 fans filled Qwest Field. The governor of Washington gave a speech. The game aired on national television. With so much excitement from Seattle, the opponent, the New York Red Bulls, didn't stand a chance.

Fredy Montero scored Seattle's first goal. The crowd roared. The Sounders scored two more times to win, 3–0.

Some of Seattle's players and coaches had taken part in games in Europe and South America, where soccer is much more popular than it is in the United States. They worried that US fans would not be as excited about the sport. But after the win against New York, Seattle assistant coach Ezra Hendrickson said, "Wow. Maybe soccer has finally arrived in America."

Fredy Montero (17) gets ready to receive a pass from teammate Brad Evans during Seattle's first-ever game.

2 OPEN CUP CHAMPIONS

Seattle's first year was a great success. Before the MLS season began, they competed in the US Open Cup, a tournament more than 100 years old. Teams from MLS and lower-level teams from the NASL and USL compete for the title. The Sounders beat the Portland Timbers, Kansas City Wizards, and Houston Dynamo to reach the finals.

In the final match, Seattle played against defending tournament champion D.C. United. The game was scoreless in the second half when Fredy Montero kicked in a goal for a 1–0 Sounders lead. Then Sebastien Le Toux passed to Roger Levesque, who slammed home the shot for a 2–0 lead. United scored in the last minute, but it wasn't enough. The Sounders won the Cup! In the MLS season, the Sounders became just the second **expansion team** to reach the playoffs, and they broke the MLS record for attendance.

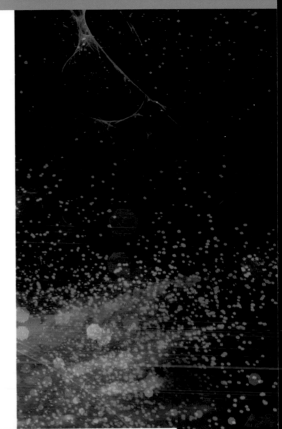

The Seattle Sounders celebrate their 2009 US Open Cup win.

Soccer fever swept through the Seattle area. For 2010, the Sounders increased their available season tickets to 32,000, and again, all the seats were sold. The season was nearly a repeat of the previous year. The Sounders won the US Open Cup again, this time at home in front of a record crowd. The winning goal came when Steve Zakuani headed a shot off the **crossbar** and Sanna Nyassi drilled the loose ball into the net. Seattle became the first MLS team ever to win back-to-back Cups. "To repeat is much tougher," said Zakuani, "and doing it at home is amazing."

Sanna Nyassi winds up to kick the ball into the net during the 2010 US Open Cup final against the Columbus Crew.

Seattle Sounders midfielder Marco Pappa celebrates a goal against the Los Angeles Galaxy.

The next year was more of the same. Seattle won its third Open Cup, this time with a 2–0 victory over the Chicago Fire at newly named CenturyLink Field. But they lost in the MLS playoffs. In 2014, they won their fourth Open Cup in six years. In MLS, they had the league's best record to claim their first **Supporters' Shield**, but they lost in the semifinal round of the playoffs.

The one missing trophy was the MLS Cup. Seattle's breakthrough came in 2016. The team won just six of its first 20 games. The Sounders replaced coach Sigi Schmid with assistant coach

Brian Schmetzer. The team responded by making the playoffs and reaching the MLS Cup final.

On a frosty field in Toronto, Ontario, the Sounders fought Toronto FC to a scoreless tie through regular time and **extra time**. The title came down to a **shoot-out**. Each team got five **direct kicks**. One of Toronto's shots clanked off the crossbar. Seattle's Roman Torres blasted his shot past goalkeeper Clint Irwin to win the title for the Sounders!

Seattle celebrates its 2016 MLS Cup win in Toronto.

SOUNDERS TIMELINE

 1996 MLS plays its first season.

 2009 Seattle plays its first season.
Seattle wins its first US Open Cup.

 2011 Seattle finishes with 63 points, the fifth
most in league history.

 2014 Seattle wins its first Supporters' Shield.
Seattle wins its fourth US Open Cup.

3 A GRAND EVENT

MLS has never been more popular. In 2016, MLS set records for average game attendance and sold-out games. The Sounders are a big reason for these records. They averaged more than 40,000 fans at games in 2016, nearly twice the league average.

Attending a Sounders match is a grand event. Before the game starts, thousands of fans gather several blocks from the stadium. The team band, Sound Wave, plays music, and the fans march to the stadium chanting the team's fight songs. Inside CenturyLink Field, fans get their faces and hair painted green and blue, the team colors. Once the game starts, fans sing and wave large banners.

Seattle's biggest regular-season games are against other MLS

SIDELINE REPORT

The Sounders are popular on the field and on the Internet. They have more than 500,000 Facebook followers and nearly as many Twitter followers.

Seattle fans wearing the team's colors cheer on their favorite team.

Seattle Sounders defender Gustav Svensson (*left*) and Vancouver Whitecaps midfielder Christian Bolanos battle for position during a 2017 match.

teams in their region—the Portland Timbers and the Vancouver Whitecaps. The team with the best record against the other two teams wins a trophy called the Cascadia Cup. Games between the Sounders and the Timbers draw crowds of well over 50,000 people.

The Sounders have had a winning record every season of their existence. And the future remains bright. With such a strong fan base supporting the team and great players and coaches on the field, the Sounders are sure to remain one of the best and most popular MLS teams for years to come.

A Seattle fan holds the Cascadia Cup before a game between the Sounders and the Timbers.

4

SEATTLE SOUNDERS

SUPER

STARS

In the Sounders' first decade in MLS, plenty of star players have emerged. Read on to learn about the best of the best.

KASEY KELLER [2009–2011]

Kasey Keller joined the Sounders at the age of 39 as a national hero. He had been the goalkeeper in four **World Cups** for the US men's national team. After playing for teams all around the world, he returned to Seattle to finish his career in the area where he grew up. His three **shutouts** to start Seattle's first season set an MLS record for longest shutout streak to start a season.

FREDY MONTERO [2009–2012]

Colombian-born speedster Fredy Montero became an instant fan favorite when he scored the first goal in Sounders history. He led the team in goals his first year, and a year later, he became the team's highest-paid player. He is still the team's all-time leading goal scorer.

OSVALDO ALONSO [2009—PRESENT]

Osvaldo Alonso is one of the best defensive midfielders in MLS history. Born in Cuba, he came to the United States when he was 21 and began playing with the Charleston Battery in 2008. He won the Rookie of the Year award before joining Seattle for its first season in 2009. Since then, he has started 247 games, scored 10 goals, and been on four MLS All-Star teams.

BRAD EVANS [2009—PRESENT]

Brad Evans came to Seattle from the Columbus Crew in 2009 and immediately became one of the team's star players. He scored the second goal in team history and started in 27 games that season. In his career with Seattle, he has been team captain and he has racked up 20 goals and 27 assists. He has also made 27 appearances with the US men's national team, and he helped the team qualify for the 2014 World Cup.

OBAFEMI MARTINS [2013–2015]

Obafemi Martins has traveled the world in a soccer uniform. He is a member of the Nigerian national team, and he has played for top teams in Italy, England, Germany, Russia, and China. His 24.7 scoring percentage (he has scored 40 goals in 162 shots) for the Sounders is the second highest in MLS history.

CLINT DEMPSEY [2013–PRESENT]

Clint Dempsey is by far the best forward ever to wear a Sounders jersey. Known as Mr. Clutch for the US national team, he has the highest scoring rate on the national team, with 0.42 goals per game. He is the first US player to score a **hat trick** in the Premier League, England's top level of professional soccer, and he is the first US player to score in three World Cups. For the Sounders, he scored the winning goal in the 2014 US Open Cup.

CHAD MARSHALL [2014—PRESENT]

Chad Marshall is the key player in Seattle's defense. He was the MLS Defender of the Year twice for the Columbus Crew before the Sounders got him in a trade. He led Seattle to the Supporters' Shield in his first year with the team and became the league's top defender for the third time. He is in the league's all-time top 10 for most games started and minutes played.

CRISTIAN ROLDAN [2015—PRESENT]

After just three seasons in professional soccer, Cristian Roldan has already established himself as a player to watch. Seattle picked him in the first round of the 2015 draft, and he started 11 games that year. It was the third most starts by a rookie in team history. In 2016, he started 34 games, and in 2017, he started all 37 games he played. He has scored 10 goals for Seattle and has been recognized as one of the best young players in MLS.

STATS STORY

The Seattle Sounders have had a winning record in MLS every year since 2009. Check out some of the team's most impressive statistics.

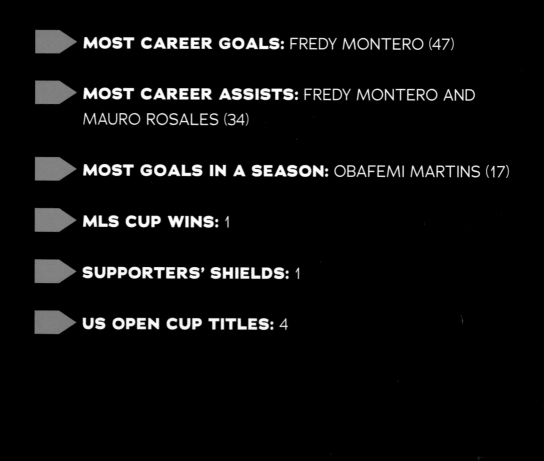

MOST CAREER GOALS: FREDY MONTERO (47)

MOST CAREER ASSISTS: FREDY MONTERO AND MAURO ROSALES (34)

MOST GOALS IN A SEASON: OBAFEMI MARTINS (17)

MLS CUP WINS: 1

SUPPORTERS' SHIELDS: 1

US OPEN CUP TITLES: 4

SOURCE NOTES

4 "Songs and Chants," Seattle Sounders FC, accessed October 10, 2017, https://www.soundersfc.com/supporters-and-alliance/supporters/songs -and-chants.

6 Stats, "Sounders Score 4 in Second Half to Beat DC United 4–3," *CBS Sports*, July 20, 2017, https://www.cbssports.com/soccer/news/sounders -score-4-in-second-half-to-beat-dc-united-4-3/.

10 ESPN staff, "Splashy Sounders Set to Kick Off in Seattle," *ESPN FC*, January 22, 2009, http://www.espnfc.com/story/611871/splashy-sounders-set-to -kick-off-in-seattle.

11 Glenn Drosendahl, "Sounders FC Makes Major League Soccer Debut on March 19, 2009," historylink.org, April 9, 2015, http://www.historylink.or g/File/11057.

14 Joshua Mayers, "Sounders FC Keeps US Open Cup," *Seattle Times*, last modified October 6, 2010, http://www.seattletimes.com/sports/sounders /sounders-fc-keeps-us-open-cup/.

GLOSSARY

crossbar: the pole across the top of the goal

direct kicks: shots taken 12 yards from the goal when a penalty is drawn or in a shoot-out

expansion team: a team that is added to a league that already exists

extra time: a 30-minute period added to the end of a match when it is tied after regular time

hat trick: three goals scored by one player in a game

MLS Cup: the trophy awarded to the season's championship team. The MLS Cup final is the championship match.

shoot-out: a way to break a tie after regulation and extra time. Each team is allowed five direct kicks that only the goalkeeper can defend. The team that scores the most goals wins.

shutouts: games in which one team does not score

Supporters' Shield: a yearly award given to the MLS team with the best regular-season record

World Cups: tournaments between the world's top national teams. The World Cup is held every four years.

FURTHER INFORMATION

Get Active with MLS
https://www.getactivewithmls.com/kids

MLS
https://www.mlssoccer.com

Rausch, David. *Major League Soccer*. Minneapolis: Bellwether, 2015.

Savage, Jeff. *Soccer Super Stats*. Minneapolis: Lerner Publications, 2018.

Seattle Sounders FC
https://www.soundersfc.com

Stewart, Mark. *Seattle Sounders F.C.* Chicago: Norwood House, 2017.

INDEX

PHOTO ACKNOWLEDGMENTS

The images in this book are used with the permission of: Icon Sportswire/Getty Images, pp. 4, 5, 6, 7, 19, 20, 21 (front fan), 27 (Roldan); Robert Giroux/Getty Images Sport, pp. 8, 11; Eugene Buchko/Shutterstock.com, p. 9; Matthew Ashton-AMA/Getty Images Sport, p. 10; Tony Quinn/MLS/Getty Images, p. 12; MCT/Tribune News Service/Getty Images, p. 13; George Holland/Cal Sport Media/Newscom, p. 14; John Green/Cal Sport Media/Alamy Stock Photo, p. 15; Claus Andersen/Getty Images Sport, pp. 16, 25 (Evans); Jim Bennett/Getty Images Sport, p. 18; Tom Hauck/Getty Images Sport, p. 21 (fans and cup); EFKS/Shutterstock.com, pp. 22–23; Bob Levey/Getty Images Sport, p. 24 (Keller); Anatoliy Lukich/Shutterstock.com, p. 24 (Montero); Gene Sweeney Jr./Getty Images Sport, p. 25 (Alonso); Victor Decolongon/Getty Images Sport, p. 26 (Martins); Photo Works/Shutterstock.com, p. 26 (Dempsey); Minas Panagiotakis/Getty Images, p. 27 (Marshall).

Cover and design elements: sakkmesterke/Shutterstock.com (fiery glow); somchaij/Shutterstock.com (soccer ball); Claus Andersen/Getty Images North America (front right); Icon Sportswire/Getty Images (front center); Photo Works/Shutterstock.com (front left); Lawkeeper/Shutterstock.com (abstract ball); Michal Zduniak/Shutterstock.com (explosion).

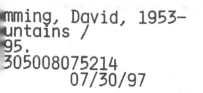
HABITATS

MOUNTAINS

DAVID CUMMING

Thomson Learning

H A B I T A T S

Deserts
Islands
Mountains
Polar Regions
Rivers and Lakes
Wetlands

Cover: The craggy snow-topped peaks of the Rocky Mountains in Canada
Contents page: The ibex spends much of its life high up above the snow line of mountain ranges in Europe and northern Africa.

First published in the United States in 1995 by
Thomson Learning
New York, NY

Published simultaneously in Great Britain by Wayland (Publishers) Ltd.

U.S. copyright © 1995 Thomson Learning

Library of Congress Cataloging-in-Publication Data
Cumming, David, 1953–
Mountains / David Cumming.
        p.   cm.—(Habitats)
    Includes bibliographical references and index.
    Summary: Describes different types of mountains and how they
are formed, the plant and animal life that exists on mountains, the
use of mountains for farming, tourism, and industry, and the efforts
to protect these unique environments.
    ISBN 1-56847-388-5 (hc)
    1. Mountains—Juvenile literature. [1. Mountains. 2. Mountain
ecology. 3. Ecology.] I. Title. II. Series.
GB512.C86   1995
551.4'32—dc20   95-18389

Printed in Italy

CONTENTS

1. THE WORLD'S MOUNTAINS

K2, or Mount Godwin Austen, in the Himalayas. This mountain is the second highest in the world.

A mountain is steep-sided highland that is at least 1,000 feet taller than the ground around it. A hill is highland that is below 1,000 feet. The peak, or summit, is the name for the top of a mountain. A mountain's height is the distance between its summit and sea level, which is usually lower than ground level. The world's highest mountain is Mount Everest, in the Himalayan range of southern Asia. Its peak is 29,028 feet above sea level.

Everest is almost certainly the highest mountain on dry land, but it is not the highest mountain on earth. This is Mauna Kea, a mountain that starts *below* sea level and whose peak juts up through the Pacific Ocean as an island in Hawaii. From its island peak to its base on the bottom of the ocean, Mauna Kea is 33,675 feet high.

An undersea mountain is called a seamount. It is completely covered by water. The tallest undersea mountain is a little lower than Everest, at 28,500 feet high. It is situated in the Pacific Ocean, between New Zealand and Samoa.

Some mountains, like Mount Kenya in east Africa, are solitary. Most mountains, however, are part of a group or chain, called a mountain range. The most important mountain ranges in the world are the Rockies of North

The world's highest peaks
The world's highest peaks (fourteen, each over 26,000 feet) are in the Himalayas in southern Asia. The five highest of these are listed below, followed by the five highest peaks in other mountain ranges.

Everest . . . .(29,028 feet)
K2 . . . .(28,250 feet)
Kanchenjunga . . . .(28,208 feet)
Lhotse . . . .(27,923 feet)
Makalu . . . .(27,790 feet)
Aconcagua, Argentina . .(22,834 feet)
McKinley, Alaska . . . . . .(20,320 feet)
Kilimanjaro, Tanzania .(19,340 feet)
El'brus, Russia . . . .(18,510 feet)
Vinson Massif, Antarctica (16,864 feet)

America, the Andes of South America, the Alps of Europe, and the Himalayas of Asia, the tallest of them all.

There are also undersea mountain ranges whose length, width, and height match all those on dry land. The Mid-Atlantic Ridge, for example, runs down the middle of the Atlantic Ocean, from near the Arctic almost to Antarctica. Its highest peaks have formed the islands of Iceland, at its northernmost point, and Bouvet, far to the south.

Mysterious, mist-shrouded mountain peaks have held a fascination for people for thousands of years.

Mountains under threat

Mountains have always fascinated people. In early times they were regarded with reverence and awe by many people, who believed that gods lived on their summits. Strange creatures were thought to lurk on

Below This map indicates the major mountain ranges of the world.

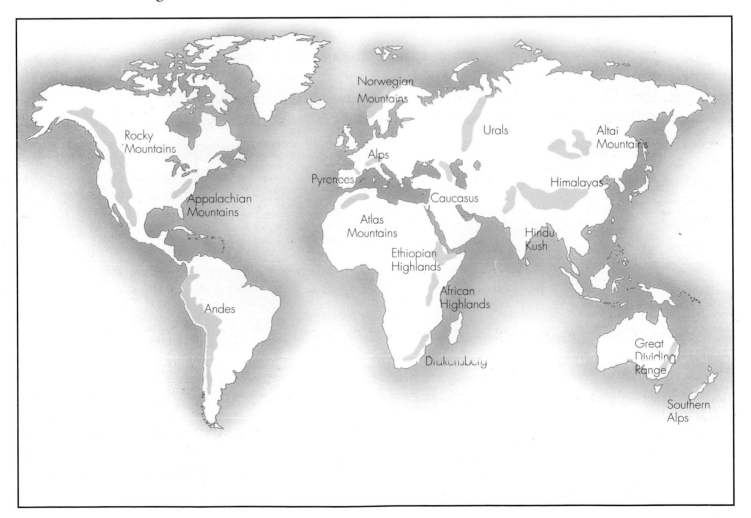

the misty slopes of the mountains and among the swirling clouds at their peaks, ready to pounce on unwary travelers. Mountains have continued to hold a religious significance in many countries, and there are many myths and legends about half-human, half-animal mountain creatures.

However, most people now no longer fear to travel in mountainous areas. Mountains have been exploited for their minerals, their water power, their forests, and their beautiful scenery, and the consequences of human interference have been disastrous.

Today, in many parts of the world, mountain environments are under threat after years of human abuse from farmers, foresters, and increasing numbers of tourists. Mountain peoples, cultures, animals, and plants have all suffered. So great has been the damage that in many parts of the world national parks have been set up to protect mountain regions. Although mountains may appear strong and enduring, they are as fragile as any other habitat, and many are in danger of being ruined forever.

The thousands of tourists who enjoy skiing on mountains all over the world are causing environmental problems.

Conquering Everest

On May 29, 1953, Edmund Hillary from New Zealand and Tenzing Norgay from Nepal were the first people to reach the top of Mount Everest, the highest point on earth. Since then, nearly five hundred people have followed in their footsteps. Ang Rita, from Nepal, has been to the summit seven times with different expeditions. Like Tenzing Norgay, he comes from the local Sherpa mountain people. In May 1992, 32 people waited in line for their turn to stand on the "roof of the world" and have their photographs taken.

Edmund Hillary took this photo of Tenzing Norgay on top of Everest.

2. HOW MOUNTAINS ARE FORMED

If you could slice the earth through the middle, you would see that it has three layers: the core, the mantle, and the crust. The core is in the earth's center, about 4,000 miles below the surface. Despite temperatures of 10,000 °F or higher, the heart of the core is kept solid by the pressure of all the rocks above it. Away from the core's heart, toward the surface, the pressure decreases and the rocks become softer, melted by the high temperatures inside the earth.

The mantle, which is 1,800 miles deep, is wrapped around the core. Currents of hot energy rise from the core to the top of the mantle, where they cool and then sink back, to heat up and rise to the top again. This keeps most of the mantle semisolid—as soft as modeling clay. However, the rocks around its rim are liquified, or molten, because there is little pressure on them and they are being heated by temperatures of nearly 10,000 °F. This molten rim, called the asthenosphere, varies in depth from 3 miles to nearly 200 miles.

The crust is around the outside of the earth. It is the layer on which we live and it "floats" on top of the molten rim of the mantle. In relation to the rest of the earth, the crust has the thickness of the skin on an apple.

The earth's crust is divided into plates that are moving constantly. Some plates are being pushed into other plates; others are being pulled apart.

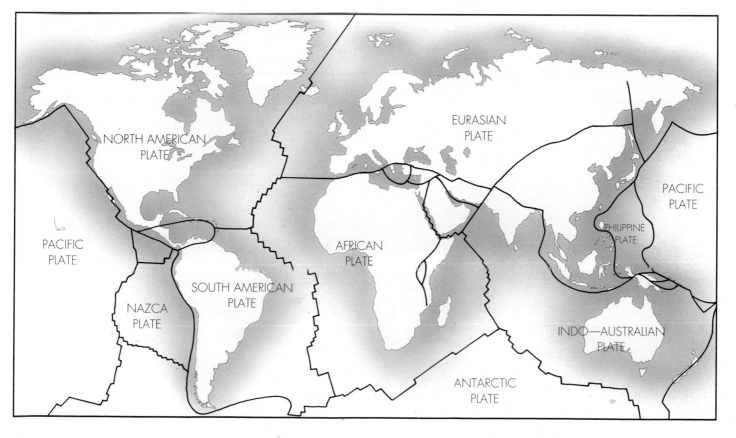

NORTH AMERICAN PLATE

EURASIAN PLATE

PACIFIC PLATE

PACIFIC PLATE

PHILIPPINE PLATE

AFRICAN PLATE

SOUTH AMERICAN PLATE

NAZCA PLATE

INDO—AUSTRALIAN PLATE

ANTARCTIC PLATE

Moving plates

Unlike the skin of an apple, the crust is not a single, continuous layer of rock. It is split up into enormous slabs, called plates, which float around in the molten asthenosphere, kept moving by the currents of heat from the mantle. The plates are of two types: oceanic and continental. These names do not refer to land and water, but to different forms of the rock within the earth's crust. Oceanic plates are made of heavy, young rocks less than 200 million years old. Continental plates contain lighter, older rocks more than 1.5 billion years old. The continental plates vary in depth from 20 to 45 miles. The oceanic plates are much thinner, only three to six miles deep in most places.

The asthenosphere's currents force neighboring plates to move apart, to move into, or just to rub against each other. In the areas where this action is most violent mountains have formed and volcanoes and earthquakes occur. The plates move very slowly, between one to four inches a year, but they have been moving since the earth was created, about 4.6 billion years ago.

Continental drift

About 200 million years ago the continents were joined together in a single area of land called Pangaea (a Greek word meaning "all-earth"), surrounded by ocean. Pangaea was like a huge jigsaw puzzle. Although locked together, its pieces were pushed and pulled by the asthenosphere's currents. Then, about 65 million years ago, the currents pulled Pangaea apart and the continents gradually drifted, over millions of years, into their present locations.

Fold mountains

Before the breakup of Pangaea, India was wedged between Africa and Asia. Following the split, the plate carrying India was pulled toward the plate carrying Asia. When the plates collided, the rocks in the seabed between

The force with which two plates collide can create fold mountains. The peaks of the folds are called anticlines, and the dips, synclines. A recumbent fold is a fold that is forced under itself into a double fold. Sometimes a fold breaks at a crack, or fault line, and is pushed forward. This is called a nappe.

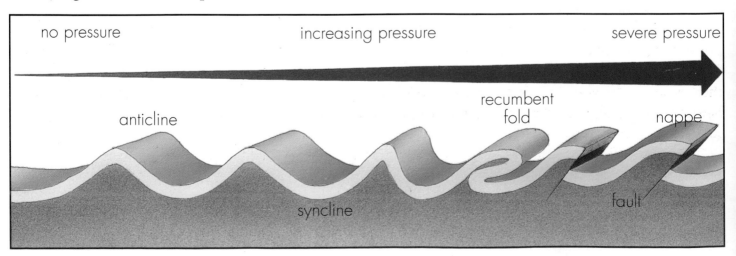

no pressure   increasing pressure   severe pressure

anticline

recumbent fold

nappe

syncline

fault

them were gradually pushed up to form the Himalayan range. We know this because fossils of sea creatures have been found high up in the Himalayas.

The Rockies, Andes, and European Alps were formed in a similar way—the Rockies by a collision between the North American plate and the Pacific plate, the Andes by the Nazca plate and the South American plate crashing into each other, and the Alps by the African and Eurasian plates colliding.

The Himalayas, Rockies, Andes, and Alps are examples of fold mountains, the name coming from the bends, or folds, in the rock strata created when the seabed was squeezed between two plates. Other fold mountains include the Atlas Mountains (north Africa), the Pyrenees (between Spain and France), and the Caucasus Mountains (between the Black Sea and Caspian Sea). The folds in them can be small or up to several miles across.

Undersea mountains

Mountains can also be created when two plates are pulled apart. Hot, molten rock (called magma) bursts through from the asthenosphere to fill the gap in the crust. The magma piles up, cools, and solidifies into mountain-high rock. The best examples of this type of mountain are on the beds of the Atlantic Ocean (the Mid-Atlantic Ridge) and Pacific Ocean (the East Pacific Rise). The Mid-Atlantic Ridge has been formed by the North and South American plates moving away from the African and Eurasian plates. Similarly, the East Pacific Rise was the result of the Pacific and Nazca plates moving apart.

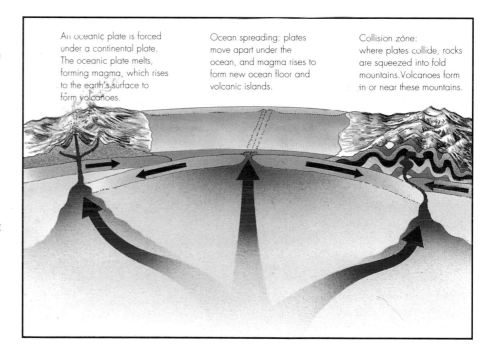

An oceanic plate is forced under a continental plate. The oceanic plate melts, forming magma, which rises to the earth's surface to form volcanoes.

Ocean spreading: plates move apart under the ocean, and magma rises to form new ocean floor and volcanic islands.

Collision zone: where plates collide, rocks are squeezed into fold mountains. Volcanoes form in or near these mountains.

A cross section of the earth's crust, showing how the plates are moved by currents in the mantle

The magma produces undersea volcanoes, which can grow tall enough for their peaks to be above sea level. Surtsey (an island south of Iceland), on the Mid-Atlantic Ridge, and Easter Island, on the East Pacific Rise, are examples of undersea volcanoes.

The new rock filling the crack in the center of the Atlantic is making new crust and pushing the plates farther apart, in a process called "ocean spreading." The Atlantic Ocean is widening in this way by almost two inches a year. However, this movement is not altering the size of the earth, because the Pacific Ocean is shrinking.

Block mountains and rift valleys

As the earth's plates have moved around, they have caused faults (cracks) in the crust. The block of land on one side of a fault can slide down the line of the fault or be pushed up it. In either case, block mountains will be the result. Most block mountains have flat tops, not pointed peaks, because they have been formed by rocks sliding up or down and not being squeezed. The Sierra Nevada Mountains in western North America are examples of block mountains.

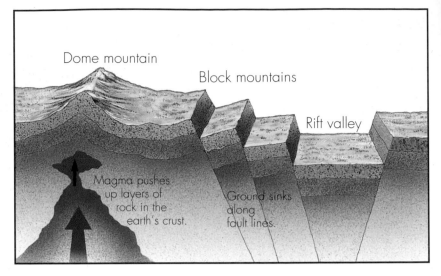

Block mountains can also be formed when two faults run parallel with each other. Again, the land in between can either be pushed up into mountains or can slip down, to leave block mountains on either side. In this case, the flat-bottomed valley between the mountains is called a rift valley, like the Great Rift Valley running through eastern Africa toward the Dead Sea, in Jordan.

Above Magma can be forced through weak points in the crust, pushing up rocks into dome mountains (see page 16). Areas of land pushed up between faults in the crust form block mountains. Rift valleys are formed when land slips down between faults.

Left Looking across the Great Rift Valley that runs through eastern Africa

10

Valleys formed by erosion

Some mountain valleys have been formed by erosion—that is, rocks being worn away naturally. Pebbles, pieces of rock, and boulders can tumble into a fast-flowing mountain stream. As they are swept downhill by the powerful current, they bounce and roll along the bed of the stream, gradually wearing it away and deepening it into a narrow V-shaped valley in the side of the mountain. These valleys may sometimes be widened by glaciers.

Above A glacier grinding its way through the Rocky Mountains of Canada

Glaciers and rivers are similar; both are water in motion, although in a glacier the water is frozen. As the glacier moves, it behaves more like a bulldozer than a river, eroding the land over which it travels. Rocks get trapped in the glacier's thick ice as it slips down a mountain valley. The ice becomes rough and, acting like a huge block of sandpaper, the glacier scrapes rock off the valley's floor and sides, making the floor flatter and wider and the sides steeper. The valley loses its original V shape and becomes a deep, U-shaped valley.

Along the coast of Norway there are deep inlets with high, steeply sloping sides. These are drowned valleys, called fjords, formed by glaciers in the last Ice Age (18,000 years ago). Much of northern Europe was covered in ice, which melted when temperatures rose at the end of the Ice Age. This caused the level of the sea to rise and flood the fjords along the Norwegian coast. Because they are deep, ships can sail along their full length. However, most fjords have shallow entrances, where the rocks that were pushed in front of a glacier were left when the ice melted, causing a moraine.

Right After being gouged by a glacier, this valley filled with seawater, to become a fjord on Norway's coast.

3. VOLCANOES AND DOME MOUNTAINS

How volcanoes occur

If a continental plate hits another continental plate, both will rise together. The Himalayas were formed in this way. However, if an oceanic plate and a continental plate collide, the oceanic plate will slide under the continental plate because it is heavier. When this happens, some of the resulting mountains might be volcanoes. The Rockies and Andes were created by a collision between oceanic and continental plates, so there are volcanoes in these mountain ranges—for example, Mount McKinley and Mount St. Helens in the Rockies, and Cotopaxi and Chimborazo in the Andes.

As the oceanic plate slides under the continental plate, it is dragged down into the rim of the earth's mantle, the asthenosphere, where the heat melts the plate's rocks, turning them into magma. The magma is pushed to the earth's surface, erupting through the crust where weak points, like folds, have been created by the movement of plates. As we have seen with undersea mountains, volcanoes can be created by plates moving apart and magma rising to fill the gap.

> **Studying volcanoes**
> *Vulcanologists are scientists who study volcanoes. They get their name—as do volcanoes—from Vulcan, the Roman god of fire. There are research stations on or near all active and inactive volcanoes, where vulcanologists keep an eye on what the volcano is doing. They use instruments that can measure what is happening inside the volcano so that people have plenty of warning before an eruption.*

Cotopaxi, in Ecuador, is the highest volcano in the world. It is 19,347 feet high.

Beneath the crust, molten rocks are called magma. When the magma bursts through the crust, it is called lava. Lava can be thick or runny when it appears and can be accompanied by clouds of gases, ash, and cinders. The hole through which all these materials appear on the earth's surface is called the crater.

Types of volcano

Most craters are at the top of the mountains (or cones) formed by volcanoes. The cones have different shapes. The commonest one—and the shape most people associate with a volcano—is a composite cone, like Mount Etna, on the island of Sicily, southern Italy. Its steep sides are made up of alternate layers of ash and lava. The ash is thrown out in violent eruptions, the lava in gentle eruptions.

Gases can build up beneath the cone and blow its top off, leaving behind a crater several miles wide. This is a called a caldera volcano. Crater Lake, in

---

Types of volcanoes

Volcanoes are classified by how often they erupt, as well as by shape. There are three types:
- *Live and active: volcanoes that erupt frequently*
- *Live and inactive: volcanoes that erupt infrequently*
- *Dead: volcanoes that will never erupt again*

At the present time there are about six hundred volcanoes that are considered to be live. The majority are inactive, but fifteen are active, emitting hot lava every month. Most of them are in countries around the Pacific Ocean, in an area known as the Ring of Fire.

Red-hot lava is blasted into the air from Kilauea, a crater on the side of Mauna Loa volcano on the island of Hawaii.

Oregon, has formed in the caldera of an extinct volcano. The Greek island of Santorini is the rim of a caldera that was flooded by the sea centuries ago.

Shield volcanoes, such as Mauna Loa in Hawaii, are created when the lava is very runny, so it covers a wide area before it solidifies. This type of volcano has long, gently sloping sides consisting of many layers of lava.

Sometimes volcanoes are formed by ash and cinders building up into a cone, like Mount Paricutin in Central America.

In Iceland, there are volcanoes that have not formed cones. Iceland is part of the Mid-Atlantic Ridge, so ocean spreading has caused cracks in the ground, some of which are 20 miles in length. Lava has been thrown out

An island is born

On November 14, 1963 some Icelandic fishermen saw bubbling and frothing in the Atlantic Ocean and great clouds of steam shooting up into the air. Although they did not know it, lava was gushing out of a crack in the Mid-Atlantic Ridge beneath them. A cone of ash 425 feet tall built up, and its peak cleared the wave tops. In April 1964, lava poured out of a hole in the peak and enclosed the ash. This quickly became solid, to form the island of Surtsey. Many other Icelandic islands have formed in this way, all because the North American and Eurasian plates are being pulled apart, causing cracks through which the asthenosphere's magma can escape.

Clouds of steam pouring from the volcano crater on Surtsey

through these cracks; it is very runny and flows great distances before it solidifies. As a result, Icelandic volcanoes have a long, low shape.

At Solfatara, near Naples, Italy, there is a volcano that has not formed a cone: its mile-wide crater is little more than a hollow in the ground. The volcano is named after the sulfur gas and steam that come out of the crater.

Like all volcanoes in Iceland, this one is low and wide.

Dome mountains

Sometimes the asthenosphere's magma does not break through the earth's crust to form a volcano. Instead, it pushes up layers of rock in the crust into a dome shape, creating dome mountains. The magma hardens into granite. When the rocks above it are worn away, the granite is exposed above the surface. The best example of dome mountains are the Black Hills in the states of South Dakota and Wyoming. Despite their name, the Black Hills reach heights of over 6,500 feet, so it is more correct to call them mountains.

Clouds of ash blown high into the skies above Mount St. Helens in Washington are carried by the wind.

The effect of volcanic ash on climate
The ash thrown out by a volcano can fall up to 60 miles away. It can also be thrown so high into the atmosphere that it will remain there for several years and affect the climate of the whole earth. In 1883, the spectacular eruption of Krakatoa, in Indonesia, sent a great amount of ash into the atmosphere. Indonesia became dark for several days because the sun could not pierce the thick cloud of dust. On the other side of the world, there were stunning sunsets in the following years, which meteorologists believed were due to dust obscuring the sun's rays.

4. WEATHER AND CLIMATE

Several factors affect the weather and climate on mountains. The most important is altitude. The higher you climb, the colder it gets, because the air becomes thinner and cannot hold as much heat as at sea level. On average, the temperature falls 1°F for every 300 feet in altitude. This is the reason why the tops of high mountains are covered with snow and ice throughout the year, even in hot countries near the equator—for instance, Kilimanjaro and Mount Kenya in East Africa.

The snow line is the height on a mountain above which there is always snow and ice. The snow line varies from region to region: in cold regions it is low—for example, at the North and South poles it is at sea level. Around the equator, however, it is 20,000 feet above sea level.

Because mountains are higher than the surrounding land, there is nothing to protect them, so they are very windy places, especially higher up their slopes. Strong winds also blow down the slopes. Cold air is heavy, so it tends to slide down the mountainsides. The steeper the mountains, the faster this cold air will drop and the sooner strong winds will develop.

The climate on a mountain varies from one side to the other. The side facing the sun will have different weather from the side in the shade. The sunny side will be warmer. Plants that like warmth will flourish here, but not on the opposite side, which is more suited to shade-loving vegetation.

The amount of rain falling on a mountainside also depends on which way the mountain is facing. When a mountain faces the prevailing wind (the windward side), it will be wet; the other side (the leeward side) will be drier.

Clouds, created when warm winds cool at high altitude, drift below the summit of Mount Cook in New Zealand's Southern Alps.

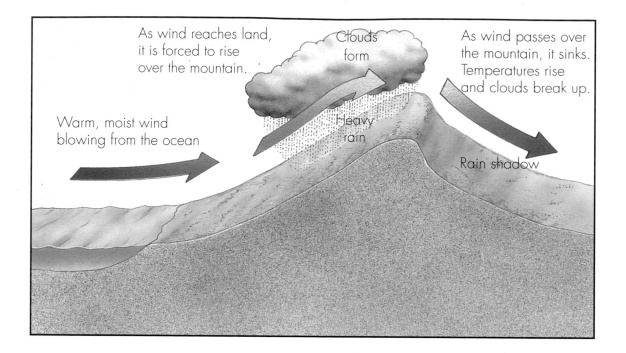

As wind reaches land, it is forced to rise over the mountain.

Clouds form

As wind passes over the mountain, it sinks. Temperatures rise and clouds break up.

Warm, moist wind blowing from the ocean

Heavy rain

Rain shadow

Left This diagram shows how mountainsides facing in the direction of rain-carrying winds receive most of the rainfall. Little rain falls on the other side of the mountain, which is in the rain shadow.

Below Even though it is near the equator, Kilimanjaro is high enough to be covered with snow all year round.

Winds blowing from the ocean are warm and moisture laden. Mountains blocking the winds' path will push them upward. As the winds rise, they are cooled. Because cold air cannot hold as much moisture as warm air, the moisture is released, falling as rain, hail, or snow on the windward side. By the time the winds descend on the leeward side of the mountain, they have lost most of their moisture, so only a little moisture will be dropped. The leeward side is said to be in the rain shadow. The eastern sides of the Rockies and the Andes, and the northern sides of the Himalayas, are rain-shadow areas.

The peaks of mountains are often shrouded by clouds. The clouds consist of droplets of water formed when the warm winds cool down as they are forced up over the mountains.

Weathering

From the moment they are created, mountains start to be destroyed by wind, rain, and ice, in a process called weathering. Strong winds wear away soft rocks, such as limestone. These rocks are also dissolved by rain water.

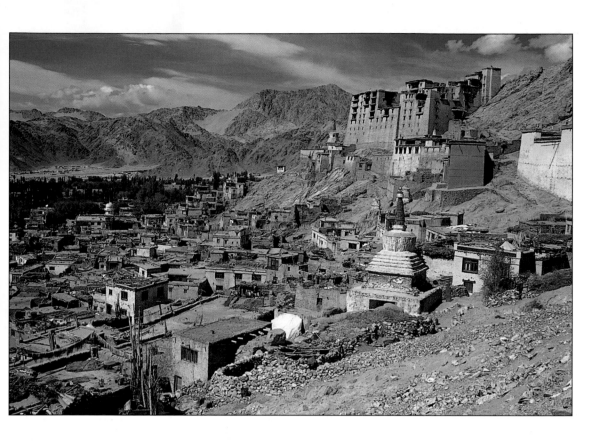

The state of Ladahk in India suffers from dry, almost desert conditions because it lies in the rain shadow of the Himalayas.

Rainwater seeps into cracks in the rocks, where it can turn into ice. As it freezes, the water expands, widening the cracks. More water can now enter the the cracks, making them even bigger when the water freezes. Eventually, this freezing and thawing splits the rocks.

The minerals inside rocks expand in the sun's heat and contract at night. In time, this expansion and contraction will cause rocks to break apart.

Vegetation flourishes on the eastern side of the Great Dividing Range in Australia. To the west is a huge desert region caused by the rain shadow.

Australia's huge rain shadow
The Great Dividing Range (or Great Divide) runs down the eastern side of Australia. Winds blowing in from the ocean are forced to drop their rain onto the eastern side of these mountains. As a result, little rain is left for the western side, which has turned into a huge desert. Little grows here, while many crops flourish to the east of the mountains, where there is plenty of rain.

5. VEGETATION

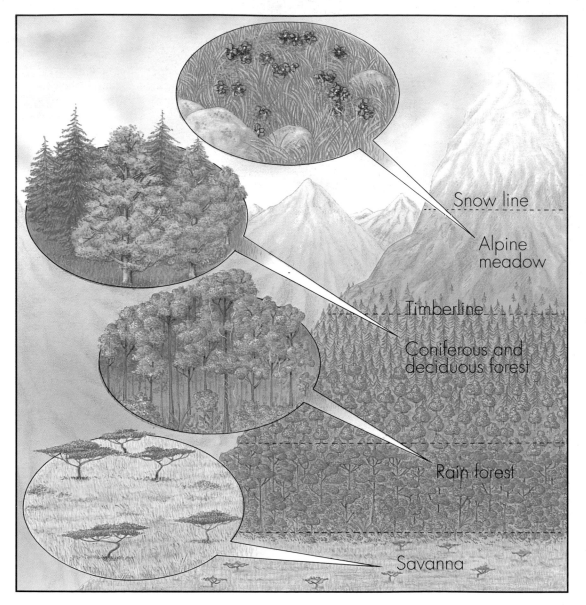

This diagram shows the different types of vegetation that can be found on a mountainside.

Snow line

Alpine meadow

Timberline

Coniferous and deciduous forest

Rain forest

Savanna

Mountain plants and trees have been forced to adapt in order to survive. Conditions vary with altitude. Plants and trees that like warmth, for example, will grow only near the foot of a mountain and will not be found higher up. Mountains can be divided into vegetation zones, according to the types of trees and plants that will grow at each level on them.

Nothing grows above the snow line because the ground is covered with snow and ice throughout the year. Below the snow line is the treeless alpine meadow zone, where short grasses, wildflowers, mosses, and lichens grow. The plants are small, with very short stems and long roots to anchor them in the soil and prevent them from being blown away by the strong winds.

In this photograph of Mount Rainier in the Rocky Mountains, we can see the alpine meadow zone just above the timberine. Above this zone there is no vegetation, while below there are forests.

To protect them from the cold, many of these plants are covered with fine hairs. The plants have bright flowers to attract the few insects that live at this altitude.

Below the alpine meadow zone is the timberline, which marks the highest point at which trees will grow on the mountain. The height of the timberline is affected by climate: it is higher in hot regions than in cold regions. Near the equator, for example, the timberline starts at 13,000 feet, but in Scandinavia it is as low as 1,600 feet.

In countries with mild climates, the timberline will be marked by evergreen conifers—trees such as spruce, fir, and pine. These trees have thick bark to protect them from the cold and needlelike leaves on which the snow and frost

Left A variety of wildflowers blooming in the summer sunshine on an alpine meadow in southern Austria

cannot settle. Below the coniferous forests are mixed forests, consisting of evergreen conifers and deciduous trees such as oak and chestnut. Finally, at the base of the mountain, there will be only deciduous trees.

In tropical countries, near the equator, the climate is too hot for coniferous forests, and the mountainsides are covered with rain forests or savanna.

Right A thick rain forest covers the lower slopes of the Darren Mountains on South Island, New Zealand.

6. WILDLIFE

The ibex, a type of wild goat, lives in the mountains of Europe, Asia, and north Africa.

Like plants and trees, mountain animals have adapted to live in their particular habitats. To keep out the cold and wind, many animals have thicker and shaggier coats than animals living in lowland regions. The hooves of sheep and goats are hard and pointed to enable them to get a good grip on steep, slippery slopes. The internal organs of mountain animals may also differ from those of lowland animals. Many have developed larger hearts and lungs to cope with the thin air at high altitudes. Yaks, a type of cattle, are so well equipped for mountain life that herds of them happily graze in the Himalayas at heights of 19,500 feet, in temperatures of -40°F.

Animals, other than insects and other tiny creatures, do not live above the alpine meadow zone. They spend the summers up there and move down in the autumn to escape the cold winters. However, some small mammals, such as snow hares and marmots, hibernate in the alpine meadow zone in winter after building up layers of fat during summer. These

Pyrenean bears
The Pyrenean brown bear, six feet tall and 450 pounds, was described in the fourteenth century as a "most common beast." Since then, thousands have been killed, until by 1937 only two hundred were left. Today, about ten still survive. These few bears roam the forested slopes of the Pyrenees Mountains between Spain and France. Although hunting them has been forbidden for many years, local shepherds continue to shoot the bears because they eat their sheep. Recently it has been agreed that shepherds will receive around $250 for every sheep killed by a bear in return for not hunting them. Also, plans exist to extend the Pyrenean National Park so that the bears can live in safety under the watchful eyes of the park rangers.

This puma is more at home in the forests at the foot of mountains than high up on the slopes.

small mammals, as well as goats and sheep, can be seen nibbling the meadows' grasses and plants. Carnivores (meat-eaters) such as wolves and pumas—and in the Himalayas, the elusive and rare snow leopard—may lurk among the rocky outcrops, ready to pounce on a grazing sheep. These creatures prefer to spend most of their time in the forests below the timberline, where there is more prey.

Mountain wildlife is most abundant in the forests on the lower slopes, especially in tropical countries, where many different types of monkeys, birds, insects, and snakes can be found.

The marmot's thick fur protects it from the cold at high altitudes.

The yeti—fact or fiction?
According to legend, the yeti is a huge, apelike creature that lives high up in the Himalayas, feeding off yaks. Some local people say the yeti is more like a human than an ape and they have nicknamed it the Abominable Snowman. Many people claim to have seen the yeti: few scientists, however, are convinced that it exists.

Mountain birds

The golden eagle is one of the largest and most common birds in the skies above all the world's mountain ranges. Powerfully built to survive this high-altitude habitat, it can easily cope with the strong gusts of wind and swirling air currents found among the peaks. Up to four feet long and fifteen pounds in weight, with a wingspan of seven feet, the golden eagle circles and soars, scanning the ground for prey with eyes ten times sharper than human eyes. Small mammals, like mountain hares, are its favorite food, and if these are in short supply, the golden eagle pounces on smaller mountain birds. Once it has spotted its victim, an eagle dives at 90 mph to grab the prey with its talons, then takes it away to a quiet spot to tear it apart with its sharp hooked beak.

Even larger than the golden eagle are the condor of the Andeas and the Californian condor. Each species usually is more than four feet long and weighs twenty pounds or more. The condor, with a wingspan of ten feet, soars above the high peaks of the Andes, ranging from the mountains to the Pacific coast. It feeds on dead animals, including huge quantities of fish. The California condor is one of the world's rarest birds—decades of hunting and trapping have nearly wiped out this species. The only hope for the survival of the species lies in catching and keeping the remaining birds in captivity, where they can breed in safety. There are plans to start releasing some of them into the wild soon, in areas where rangers can keep a careful watch on them.

A condor gliding among the peaks of the Andes Mountains in South America

A bald eagle flying high above the Rockies

The bald eagle
This is a very large type of sea eagle, measuring about three feet in length. Bald eagles have high arched beaks and bare legs. They are found only in North America and have become the national emblem of the United States. They feed on fish from rivers and lakes and are often found in mountainous regions of North America. Bald eagles were once hunted and killed in the thousands, especially in Alaska, where they caused problems for fishermen because they ate salmon.

7. MOUNTAIN PEOPLE

In the same way that plants and animals have adapted to their mountain habitats, so have mountain people. Lowland visitors to mountains above 10,000 feet often suffer from "altitude sickness"—breathlessness, light-headedness, and headaches. This is because the air, being thinner, contains less oxygen: above 10,000 feet, people take in with each breath about half the amount of oxygen that they take in at sea level. Mountain peoples, such as the Sherpas of Nepal and the Aymara Indians of South America, do not suffer from altitude sickness. This is because they have larger lungs to take in more oxygen, more blood cells to carry the oxygen, and larger hearts to pump the blood quickly around their bodies than do people living in the lowlands.

Because mountain air is thin, more of the sun's harmful rays can pass through it. As a result, many mountain peoples have developed tough, dark skin that is not easily burned by the sun. Fair-skinned lowlanders need sunscreen to protect them from sunburn when they come to the mountains.

These Sherpa women of Nepal cannot afford animals, so they have to carry everything themselves.

These Aymara women live in the Andes Mountains. They earn little money from farming, so they make clothes to sell in the markets.

A tough life

Mountain people are usually among the poorest of the population in most countries. It is not easy to build roads and railroads in mountainous areas, so communication is often difficult for many mountain people, who are frequently cut off from the rest of their country. As a result, some mountain communities have been almost forgotten by their governments, which may give them very little support and assistance.

Cut off from the rest of India by the Himalayas, the state of Ladakh has had little assistance from the Indian government in providing modern facilities.

A mountain civilization

Most of the world's oldest civilizations developed on the plains, where life was easier than in the mountains. The Incas, a mountain people of South America, were the exception. Their great empire lasted from A.D. 1100 to the 1500s, and it was ruled from Cuzco (in modern-day Peru), 11,500 feet up in the Andes Mountains. Another important Inca city was Machu Picchu, which was built at a height of 7,800 feet in the Andes.

Machu Picchu, once an important city of the Inca Empire

While lowland areas have progressed, mountain towns and villages have usually developed more slowly. They have been the last places to get electricity, telephones, television, clean drinking water, new schools, hospitals, and factories. In mountain communities in developing countries, there are usually fewer facilities and job opportunities than in the lowlands. In the mountain regions of India and in Nepal, for example, many men are forced to leave their villages to earn money in the lowlands. Some of them join the army and send most of their earnings home. In their absence, family farms are run by the men's parents, wives, and children. The men try to take their vacations at busy times of the year, such as when their crops need harvesting.

In addition to these problems, mountain people have to cope with a harsh climate. Daily life is a struggle, which has made them much hardier than lowlanders. Often isolated, and ignored by their governments, they have become independent, resourceful people who can look after themselves.

The people in this Nepalese village have stripped the land of all its trees, so the soil will soon become eroded.

The Gurkha people of Nepal, for example, served as soldiers in the British Army for many years. They have impressed the British with their resourcefulness, stamina, and fighting skills. Similarly, the Pathan peoples, who live in the mountains of northwest Pakistan, have always provoked fear and dread in their enemies. Even today, the government of Pakistan allows the Pathans to run their own affairs and does not risk offending them by passing laws that they would not approve.

The Afghan guerrilla troops from the mountains of Afghanistan were the toughest fighters in the war between Afghanistan and the Soviet Union, which was fought in the 1980s.

The effects of deforestation on people

Mountain people often have large families. They need their children to help with farming or to earn money by going out to work. There is often a poor standard of health care in mountain communities, leading to a high death rate among children. This is another reason why mountain people have large families. In one mountain country, Nepal, the population has more than quadrupled in the last forty years. To feed all these people, more farmland has been provided by cutting down trees and clearing huge areas of forest. This is called deforestation. People have also cut down trees and sold the wood for fuel. In the 1940s, 60 percent of Nepal was covered with forests; today only 30 percent of the land is forest.

Deforestation has affected the people in many ways. Trees protect the soil from heavy rain, and their roots help to hold the soil and stop it from being washed away. The cutting down of the forests means that the already poor mountain soil is washed off the land and drains into rivers, blocking them and causing flooding.

An Indian holy man among the forests of the Himalayas

Mountains and religion

Mountains have always been quiet, peaceful places—perfect for holy people who do not want to be troubled by the noise and temptations of daily life. Ancient peoples believed that the mountains were the home of their gods. The ancient Greeks, for example, believed their gods lived on top of Mount Olympus, in Greece. According to the Hindu holy books, Hindu gods live in the Himalayas, and one of the most sacred rivers in India, the Ganges rises there. Thousands of Hindus make pilgrimages to shrines in the Himalayas. In the Mount Athos area of northern Greece, monks have built twenty monasteries in the mountains, and the only way to reach many of them is to be hauled up in a large basket.

8. FARMING

Without terraces, these Himalayan farmers would have no flatland on which to grow crops.

Most mountain people live by farming. The majority of them are subsistence farmers. This means that their farms can produce enough food for the family, but little is left over for sale in a market. Even if they have surplus food, the isolation of their farms makes it difficult for them to get their produce to market.

In many countries, mountain farmers have leveled the land by building steps, or terraces, up the slopes of the mountains. They edge the terraces with stone walls, which help to prevent the rain from washing away the soil.

Left Farmers in the Andes Mountains of South America breed llamas for their wool.

Mountain soil is poor for growing crops because it is thin and rocky. Crops grown in mountain areas include cereals, fruits, and vegetables in temperate countries and coffee and bananas in tropical lands.

Except in developed countries, few mountain farmers have money to buy machines or even good-quality tools, so most of the work is done by hand, with animals being used to pull plows and carts. Even in developed countries, the slopes are often so steep that the farmers can use only the smallest machines.

The rearing of animals is an important feature of mountain farming. In temperate mountain regions such as the European Alps, the mountains of Scandinavia, and the Rockies of North America, the livestock reared is mainly dairy cattle, sheep, and goats. In winter, the animals are kept on the lower slopes, housed in barns during the coldest periods. In summer, farmers may take their animals up to graze on the nourishing grasses and plants of the alpine meadows. Sometimes the farmer will be accompanied up the slopes by his whole family, who will spend the summer in their mountain home. They will harvest the dried grass (hay) to feed the animals in winter and

Below This Himalayan farmer uses a type of yak called a dzo to pull his plow.

32

In summer, the hay is cut and cattle are grazed in these alpine meadows in Switzerland. In winter, the meadows are buried beneath thick snow.

may make dairy products, including butter and cheese. In the autumn, the family and animals return to the lower slopes, where they will spend the winter. This annual movement of farmers and animals is called transhumance.

In other mountain regions, different animals are reared, such as yaks in the Himalayas and llamas in the Andes of South America. These animals are used for carrying goods, pulling farm equipment, and providing meat and milk for food or wool and hides for clothing.

Many uses of a yak

Some mountain animals have been domesticated by farmers. A yak, for instance, can be used for:

- *pulling a plow*
- *carrying heavy loads*
- *providing milk for drinking and making into butter*
- *providing skins for clothes, blankets, and floor rugs*
- *providing dung, which can be used as a fertilizer and as fuel*

This team of yaks in Nepal is being used to carry people and equipment on a climbing expedition.

9. INDUSTRY, TOURISM, AND POWER

Mines and quarries

Most mountain ranges have been formed by enormous upheavals in the earth's crust. Their rocks have experienced terrific pressures and high temperatures, which have changed them. For example, soft limestone has been squeezed into hard marble and crumbly shales (fine rocks) into brittle slate. Italy's Apennine Mountains are famous for the quarries where marble has been removed for centuries. The marble is used in buildings and for sculptures.

During the formation of mountains, hot, molten magma from the asthenosphere has oozed up into the rocks to settle in the gaps and cracks between them. Here the magma has cooled into "veins" of useful or rare minerals. Gold, silver, and platinum may be found. However, most of the minerals are mixed with others to form mineral ores, such as iron ore and zinc ore. Mines are dug into the mountainsides so that these

A copper mine in the mountains of Mexico

The lure of gold
Mountain streams often flow over veins of mineral ores and wash tiny pieces of them down to the plains. The discovery of gold in streams from the Rockies led to "gold rushes" in North America at the end of the nineteenth century. One of the most famous was the Klondike Gold Rush, to the Klondike River in the Yukon, northwest Canada, in 1896–98. Thousands of gold prospectors left their homes and traveled huge distances in the hope of making their fortunes. Few became rich; many died. Today, ghost towns are all that remain of those exciting times.

A mountain of silver

Potosí is a town 13,700 feet above sea level in the Andes Mountains in Bolivia. It was built at the foot of the 15,380-foot-high Cerro Potosí, which is famous for its silver ore. In the 1500s, Spanish conquistadores (conquerors) discovered the mountain when they invaded the region now called Bolivia and brought it into the Spanish Empire. By the end of the eighteenth century, huge amounts of silver had been taken and the Spaniards left Potosí, believing that they had removed all the mountain's silver.

Some ten thousand miners now work in the five hundred tunnels dug into Cerro Potosí. It is dangerous work, and they earn low wages because only low-quality silver ore remains.

The entrance to one of the ancient silver mines founded by the Spaniards. Here miners still dig for silver deep in the Cerro Potosí mountain in Bolivia.

riches can be extracted. Sometimes the ores lie close to the surface, so strip-mining is used rather than digging deep into the ground.

Forestry

In some mountain regions forestry is an important industry. On the slopes of the Rocky Mountains in the United States and Canada are softwoods, such as spruce, pine, and aspen, which are used for building. In the Appalachian Mountains, in the eastern United States, there are hardwood forests, where timber is cut down and used for many purposes.

Many countries now limit the number of trees that can be cut down for timber.

Valuable hardwood trees such as teak, mahogany, and ebony grow in mountain forests in many tropical regions of the world. Timber may be taken from these forests, but in many countries it is against the law to cut down trees in mountainous regions because of mudslides and other damage resulting from the loss of forests.

Tourism

In almost all mountainous areas the most valuable resource does not lie below the ground, but on top of it. This is the landscape itself. Tourism is now one of the most important industries in mountain regions. People come from far away to enjoy the often spectacular scenery, breathe the clean air, and take part in pastimes and sports ranging from walking and sightseeing to more energetic activities such as skiing, climbing, and mountain biking.

To cater to the tourists' needs, hotels, restaurants, cable cars, stores, and ski lifts have to be built and people employed to operate them. Tourism brings jobs into an area where they are hard to find. The jobs are usually year-round, since many people visit the mountains in the summer as well as in the winter. There is plenty to do there all year.

Above Rock climbing is a very popular mountain sport in the summer months when the snow has melted.

Right A team of mountain walkers enjoying the clean air and beautiful scenery

However, tourism can be very damaging to mountain areas. Walkers and bikers, for example, wear away paths and leave garbage. In Nepal, it is said that you do not need a map to get to Everest: just follow the trail of soda cans and candy wrappers left by others. Tourists in Nepal have contributed to the deforestation of the Himalayas. Many people go hiking in the hills and mountains and stay at guest houses owned by local people. As the number of visitors increase, the need for cooking and heating fuel grows, so more trees are chopped down. Trees are also needed for building guest houses and other facilities for tourists.

In isolated mountain regions, tourists can bring disease, or they may introduce customs that disturb the local people's traditional way of life—for example, some tourists wear shorts or bikinis where the local people are Muslims, who believe the body should be covered.

Skiing is an important part of the winter tourist industry in the French Alps.

Hydroelectric power

Falling water produces power that can be used to turn turbines, connected to generators, to make electricity. Mountain rivers are ideal for generating hydroelectricity because they are very powerful as they thunder down the steep slopes to the plains. Dams containing turbines can be built across these rivers to make use of their power. Dams can also be built across rivers in mountain valleys so that reservoirs (artificial lakes) build up behind them.

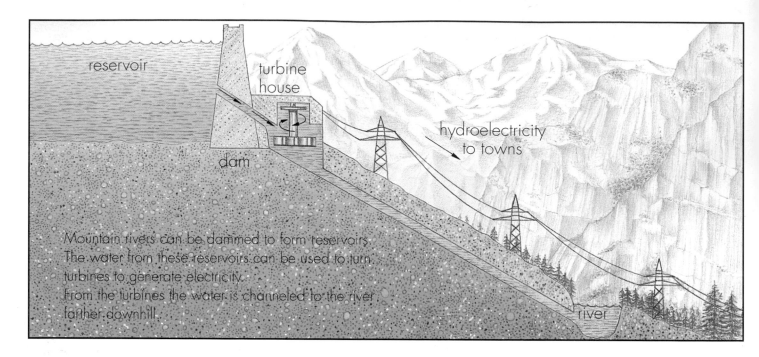

reservoir

turbine house

dam

hydroelectricity to towns

river

Mountain rivers can be dammed to form reservoirs. The water from these reservoirs can be used to turn turbines to generate electricity. From the turbines the water is channeled to the river farther downhill.

When the water empties out of the reservoir, it can be used to drive turbines. Mountainous countries like Switzerland and Norway generate most of their electricity in this way.

Dams and hydroelectric power stations are costly, but once they have been built, they produce electricity very cheaply. This is an environmentally friendly way of making electricity because no harmful fossil fuels are involved. However, if a reservoir has to be created, then the environment is affected because thousands of acres of land are flooded by its waters, perhaps causing farms or even villages to be moved and destroying the habitat for wildlife.

This diagram shows how the power of falling water can be used to generate hydroelectricity.

Using the Snowy River

The Snowy River flows down the eastern side of the Great Dividing Range in Australia. Its fast-flowing waters are used for hydroelectricity and for irrigation. Sixteen dams and nine power stations have been built on the river. In addition, 100 miles of pipes divert river water to irrigate farms situated in the rain shadow on the west of the mountains. This region was previously too dry for growing crops, but now, with irrigation, they can be planted.

One of the dams used for hydroelectricity on the Snowy River in Australia

10. TRANSPORTATION PROBLEMS

In the past mountains formed a barrier for people. They could be crossed only by traveling through the passes between valleys. The passes could be used in summer, but not in winter, when they were often blocked by deep snow, and the paths leading up to them were treacherous with ice. Even if the passes were free from snow in winter, bitterly cold temperatures made travel across them impossible.

Today, in developed countries, mountains are no longer great obstacles to travel, although some high passes can still be closed in winter. Planes and helicopters can fly over even the highest mountains. Long tunnels for trains and vehicles, such as the Simplon and St. Gotthard tunnels in the Alps, have been cut through many mountain barriers. Roads zigzag up one side of mountain ranges and down the other—for example, the Karakoram Highway through the Karakoram mountain range, leading from Pakistan into China.

This tunnel through the Alps makes it easier to travel between Switzerland and Italy.

Most developing countries, however, do not have the money to build transportation routes through mountainous areas. Often there are no roads, only tracks just wide enough for a horse or donkey laden with food or firewood to struggle up. Sometimes there are only footpaths that are too narrow even for animals. Then people have to carry heavy sacks of grain or water containers on their backs to take to their homes.

Landslides and avalanches

Landslides frequently occur on mountains. On steep slopes, rocks and soil may be loosened by heavy rain and wind and sent crashing downhill. Roads can be blocked and villages cut off for weeks while all the material is cleared away. Deforestation makes the problem worse because the soil is washed off the mountainsides more easily by heavy rain. In 1920 there was a terrible landslide in China that killed at least 180,000 people.

Left A large mass of snow pours down a mountainside in the French Alps. Avalanches are constant threats to people and property in mountainous areas.

Mountain porters crossing a stream in the Himalayas. In a treacherous place like this, humans are better able than animals to carry goods.

Landslides are sometimes caused by earthquakes, which are common in mountainous areas. As we have already seen, mountains have formed in places where the crust's plates are moving. As they bump and grind against each other, vibrations may be sent through the layers of rock, causing the ground above to shake. The shaking may dislodge huge chunks of mountainside, sending it tumbling into the valley below.

In winter, communications in mountain areas can be disrupted by avalanches, which close roads and destroy telephone lines. An avalanche is a large mass of snow that slips down a mountainside, knocking down and burying everything in its way. Avalanches are started by vibrations—these may be caused by an earthquake or earth tremor, or even a loud noise, like a gunshot or shouting. In areas where avalanches occur often, strong fences are built and forests planted to try to stop the speed and distance of the avalanche's destruction.

Truck pollution in Switzerland

In February 1994, the people of Switzerland voted against foreign trucks traveling across their country. Gases from truck exhausts are one reason for acid rain, which has killed an alarming number of trees on Swiss mountainsides. Without the trees' roots to hold it together, the soil slides down the slopes more easily and causes damage to villages. The Swiss government plans to build two new rail tunnels through the Alps, which will allow trains to transport 3 million trucks a year across Switzerland, so that the trucks will not need to use the country's roads.

11. CONSERVATION FOR THE FUTURE

Mountains under threat

Tall and mighty, mountains certainly do not appear weak and easily damaged. In fact, as we have seen, they are readily harmed and are under constant attack from nature and from humans.

Beneath the earth's crust, strong currents within the asthenosphere continue to move the plates, which can lead to earthquakes. Then huge chunks of mountainside may be dislodged and disappear into the valleys.

Taller than the surrounding land, mountains are unprotected from the worst of the weather. They receive the full force of wind and rain, both of which wear away the mountain's rocky exterior. The Himalayas, for example, are among the world's youngest mountains. Their rocks are still relatively soft compared to those on older mountains. In every square mile, 2,500 tons of rock are being worn away each year.

Although Mount Everest, the world's highest mountain, looks strong and enduring, it is actually soft and easily eroded by the weather.

Humans are adding to the destruction of the Himalayas, which were once covered with forests on their lower slopes. Today, many of the mountainsides in developing countries are bare, their trees chopped down for fuel, for building materials, and for making furniture. The grass on many of their pastures is very thin, because too many goats and sheep have been allowed to graze on them without giving the grass enough time to grow. The roots of the trees and grass helped prevent the soil from being blown away by the wind and washed downhill by the rain. Without their protection, a lot of soil is lost every year. As the soils become thin and poor, farmers start cutting down more trees to sell because they cannot earn anything from their land. And so the damage continues—and worsens.

In many wealthy mountain countries, human pollution—from industry and car and truck exhausts—is causing acid rain that is destroying whole forests.

Little will grow on this deforested hillside in India because the soil is now very thin and rocky.

People are also harming the mountains by visiting them. Tourists are wearing away paths, uprooting plants, frightening the wildlife, and leaving behind garbage that is nonbiodegradable. This is even a problem on Mount Everest because many big expeditions come every year to climb it . Now climbers have to bring down everything they take up—unless it is biodegradable, in which case it can be buried to rot away.

Tourism is also encouraging people to abandon farm work. Many farmers' children prefer to work in hotels, restaurants, or stores, where they can earn more money than from farming. As a result, mountain land is neglected and becomes ruined.

Some conservation solutions

Nothing can be done to stop nature's destruction of mountains. Humans, however, can reduce the amount of harm they do to them.

Already, many countries have opened special mountain parks, where humans interfere as little as possible with the landscape and animals. Rangers keep a careful eye on the people to ensure that they abide by the rules. Visitors may have to pay large fines if they are caught disturbing the animals or dropping trash.

In developing countries, government officials are being trained to visit mountain villages to give advice on improving farming methods. They advise against over-grazing pastureland and also encourage families to open handicraft workshops to earn money as an alternative to cutting down trees. The governments themselves are trying to spend more money in mountain areas so that there are better facilities for the local people, in the hope that fewer will move away to the lowlands or to work in the tourist industry.

Many developing countries are unsure about tourism. On the one hand it brings them much-needed money and provides many jobs. On the other hand, it can do a lot of harm—not only to the environment, but to local ways of life and cultures. The small Himalayan kingdom

Above Much of this garbage in the Himalayas has been dropped by tourists.

Some of the unspoiled forests of the Himalayan Kingdom of Bhutan, which could be destroyed by tourism.

of Bhutan has decided that tourism does more harm than good. Only a few foreigners are allowed to visit the country each year, and they have to pay a large fee before they are allowed in. In this way, Bhutan earns a lot of money from a few tourists. Bhutan's neighbor, Nepal, however, does not limit the number of tourists allowed in, and thousands of people go there every year to walk along its mountain paths. The tourists have to buy a special permit to do this, and the money is used to clean up the mess made by walkers and to repair the damage done to paths by all their boots. However, Nepal tries to restrict the number of climbers on Mount Everest by charging them a very high fee for permission to climb the mountain. Every climbing expedition has to pay $10,000 per person.

All over the world, in both developed and developing countries, there is a growing awareness of the need to protect mountain areas so that future generations can enjoy them as much as we do.

Mount McKinley, the highest mountain in North America, photographed from Denali National Park in Alaska. Great care is taken in national parks such as this to ensure that the beautiful scenery is not harmed by tourists.

45

Glossary

Acid rain   Rain that contains chemicals that can damage plants, animals, and buildings, absorbed from factory smoke and traffic exhaust fumes.

Alpine   Relating to high mountains.

Altitude   The height above sea level.

Conifers   Evergreen trees with cones.

Conservationists   People who try to protect the environment from being harmed.

Core   The center of the earth.

Crust   The outside of the earth, on which we live.

Deciduous trees   Trees that lose their leaves in winter.

Deforestation   The cutting down and clearance of trees from land.

Elusive   Difficult to see or catch.

Environment   The surroundings in which humans, animals, and plants live.

Evergreen trees   Trees that keep their leaves all year.

Exploitation   To use up resources without thinking about the consequences.

Extinct   No longer active or living.

Fossils   The remains or traces of animals and plants.

Fossil fuels   Naturally occurring fuels, such as coal, oil, peat, and natural gas, that have been formed by the decaying of organic matter.

Foothills   The smaller hills along the edge of a mountain range.

Habitat   The place where a species of animal or plant lives naturally.

Hibernate   To spend the winter in a deep sleep.

Hydroelectricity   Electricity generated by the power of falling water.

Ice Age   A period in history when much of the earth was covered with ice. The last Ice Age was about 18,000 years ago.

Irrigation   Supplying farmland with water through a system of canals, channels, and pumps.

Lava   Molten rock from the mantle that comes out of cracks in the earth's crust.

Magma   Molten rocks beneath the earth's crust.

Mantle   The layer between the earth's crust and core.

Minerals   Naturally occurring substances in rocks and soil.

Molten   Melted, liquefied by high temperatures.

Moraine   A mass of debris such as soil and rocks, carried by a glacier and forming ridges and mounds when it is deposited.

National parks   Areas of countryside in which the wildlife and scenery are protected.

Nonbiodegradable   Something that does not rot naturally.

Pass   Lowland between mountains which people use to travel through mountainous areas.

Plates   Large moving sections of the earth's crust.

Persecution   Attacking a person for his or her religious beliefs.

Prevailing wind   The direction from which a wind usually comes.

Reservoir   A lake created by a dam across a river.

Soviet Union   A former group of republics in Eastern Europe and Western Asia that broke up into separate states in 1991.

Species   A group of animals or plants that are very similar or related and can reproduce.

Strata   Layers of rocks.

Strip-mining   Mining by digging down from the surface rather than tunneling underground. Also called opencast mining.

FURTHER READING

Amsel, Sheri. *Mountains.* Habitats of the World. Milwaukee: Raintree Steck-Vaughn, 1992.

Burns, Diane. *Rocky Mountain Seasons: From Valley to Mountaintop.* New York: Macmillan Children's Books, 1993.

Booth, Basil. *Earthquakes and Volcanoes.* Repairing the Damage. New York: New Discovery Books, 1992.

Bullen, Sue. *The Alps and Their People.* People and Places. New York: Thomson Learning, 1994.

Collinson, Alan. *Mountains.* Ecology Watch. New York: Dillon Press, 1991.

Dixon, Dougal. *The Changing Earth.* Young Geographer. New York: Thomson Learning, 1993.

Fleisher, Paul. *Ecology A to Z.* New York: Dillon Press, 1994.

Snedden, Robert. *The Super Science Book of Rocks and Soils.* Super Science. New York: Thomson Learning, 1994.

Wiggers, Raymond. The Amateur Geologist: Explorations and Investigations. Amateur Science. New York: Franklin Watts, 1993.

Other sources of information are travel and geography books about specific mountain ranges such as the Himalayas, the Appalachians, or the Vosges Mountains in France. It is also worth looking at books about geology for more information on how mountains form and what they are made of.

FURTHER INFORMATION

For further information about animals and their habitats that are under threat, contact the following environmental organizations:

Center for Environmental Education, Center for Marine Conservation, 1725 De Sales Street NW, Suite 500, Washington, DC 20036

Friends of the Earth (U.S.A.), 218 D Street SE, Washington, D.C. 20003

Greenpeace U.S.A., 1436 U Street NW, Washington, DC 20009

World Wildlife Fund, 1250 24th Street NW, Washington DC 20037

These organizations all campaign to protect wildlife and habitats throughout the world.

Picture acknowledgments
Britstock-IFA cover,/Tetsuo Sayama 17(lower); David Cumming 19(top), 27(lower), 30, 32(lower); Eye Ubiquitous /L.Fordyce 11(top), 21(top), /J.B.Pickering 39, /D.Cumming 40, /J.Waterlow 41(top); Hutchison Library 27(top), J.Horner 35(top); Frank Lane Picture Agency /Silvestris iii & 23, /L.Lee Rue 24(top), /C.Mullen 31, /T.Wharton 33; NHPA /B.Hawkes 15(top), /J.Meech 22(lower), /J.Shaw 35(lower), /38, /N.A.Callow 41(lower); Royal Geographical Society 6(lower), Still Pictures /M. Edwards 5, /R.Van der Giessen 12, /D.Decobecq 13, /M.& C.Denis Huot 17(top), /Udo Hirsch 28, /J.Etchart 29, 32(top), /45; Tony Stone Worldwide /J.Noble 4, /R.Elliot 6(top), A.Husmo ii 11(lower), G.Vaughan 14, /B.Parsley 15(lower), /S.Huber 22(top), /D.J.Cox 24(centre), C.Prior 26, /L.Lefkowitz 34, /J.McBride 36(top), /D.Smetzer 36(lower), /N.DeVore 42, /44(top), Zefa /Armstrong 16.
Artwork on pages 5, 7, 8, 9, 10, 18 by Peter Bull, and on pages 20 and 38 by John Yates.

INDEX

Numbers in **bold** refer to photographs.